The Ancient Greek ECONOMY

Henry Bensinger

Published in 2014 by The Rosen Publishing Group, Inc.
29 East 21st Street, New York, NY 10010

First Edition

Editor: Joanne Randolph
Book Design: Kate Vlachos

Photo Credits: Cover Hoberman Collection/Universal Images Group/Getty Images; p. 5 Leemage/ Universal Images Group/Getty Images; p. 6 Maria Yfanti/Shutterstock.com; p. 7 farbled/ Shutterstock.com; p. 8 Greek School/The Bridgeman Art Library/Getty Images; p. 9 Paul Picone/ Shutterstock.com; pp. 10, 12, 13, 19, 21 (left) DEA/G. Dagli Orti/De Agostini Picture Library/Getty Images; p. 11 Werner Forman/Universal Images Group/Getty Images; p. 14 Hemera Technologies/ PhotoObjects.net/Thinkstock; p. 15 Andrei Nekrassov/Shutterstock.com; p. 16 Alberto Pizzoli/ AFP/Getty Images; pp. 17, 21 (right) DEA/G. Nimatallah/De Agostini/Getty Images; p. 18 Dennis K. Johnson/Lonely Planet Images/Getty Images; p. 20 Antonio Abrignani/Shutterstock.com; p. 22 Lefteris Papaulakis/Shutterstock.com.

Library of Congress Cataloging-in-Publication Data

Bensinger, Henry.
 The ancient Greek economy / by Henry Bensinger. — First Edition.
    pages cm — (Spotlight on ancient civilizations: Greece)
 Includes index.
 ISBN 978-1-4777-0771-5 (library binding) — ISBN 978-1-4777-0875-0 (pbk.) —
 ISBN 978-1-4777-0876-7 (6-pack)
 1. Greece—Economic conditions. 2. Greece—History. 3. History, Ancient. I. Title.
 HC293.B46 2014
 330.938—dc23
                              2012051000

Manufactured in the United States of America

CPSIA Compliance Information: Batch #S13PK2: For Further Information contact Rosen Publishing, New York, New York at 1-800-237-9932

CONTENTS

Farming in Ancient Greece

The people who made up ancient Greek **civilization** lived in Greece from about 750 BC to around 500 AD. Most of the people in ancient Greece worked as farmers. Farming was not easy in Greece, though. The climate was hot and dry for half the year and humid with little rain for the other half. The poor soil was rocky, so many crops would not grow.

The Greeks had the best success growing barley. They grew some wheat, as well. Olives and grapes were the other main crops. Grapes were used to make wine. Olives were used in cooking and also for their oil.

Around 80 percent of Greek citizens were farmers. Here Greek farmers are harvesting olives. Olive oil could be used to make perfumes and soaps, among other things.

Mining

Greece's rocky land had a benefit. There were many deposits of metal **ore** under the ground. Some of the most well-known mines in ancient Greece were the silver mines in Laurium, near Athens. There were many iron, gold, and copper mines, too.

These ruins are in Laurium, also called Lavrion, which was one of the mining centers in ancient Greece.

It took a lot of work to dig mines and find silver and other metals. There were around 20,000 slaves working in the Laurium mines at its height.

The Greeks used these metals to make sculptures, tools, pots, weapons, and other goods. These goods were useful for the people of Greece. They were also useful to trade with other places for goods that the Greeks could not grow or make themselves.

Ancient Greek Currency

Greek coins, such as this Athenian drachma, were made in a mint. A worker placed the metal between two molds on an anvil. Then he hammered the molds, which gave the coin its shape.

In the earliest days of ancient Greece, there was no money, or **currency**. Instead the Greeks traded, or bartered, for what they needed.

By 500 BC, though, most city-states had their own coins. Athens often had an owl on its coins, as a

symbol of Athena and their city. Some Greek coins had images of barley on them. This was because barley was such an important part of the economy.

The first Greek coins were called drachmas. They were made of silver. Greeks also made coins from a mix of silver and gold.

This Athenian coin had the head of a soldier printed on it. This coin is made of silver.

So Many Jobs

There were no machines like the ones we use today to make things or complete tasks in ancient Greece. People made the things they needed by hand. Many Greeks were **artisans**. They learned their crafts from

Artisans made the things people used each day. Weavers, such as these women, made cloth that could be used for clothing.

This carving shows a shoemaker in ancient Greece. People mainly wore leather sandals at this time.

their fathers. Crafts included carpentry, sculpting, metalworking, pottery making, and leatherworking. It took years to become an expert in these skills.

Not everyone in ancient Greece was an artisan. Some were builders, helping to construct temples, forts, and roads. Some people fished for a living. Some were soldiers or officials. There were many jobs to do in ancient Greece.

Making Pottery

Different parts of Greece became known for the products they made. For example, Kerameikos, which was part of Athens, was known for **ceramics**. The people there made roof tiles, statues, large sculptures, and pottery.

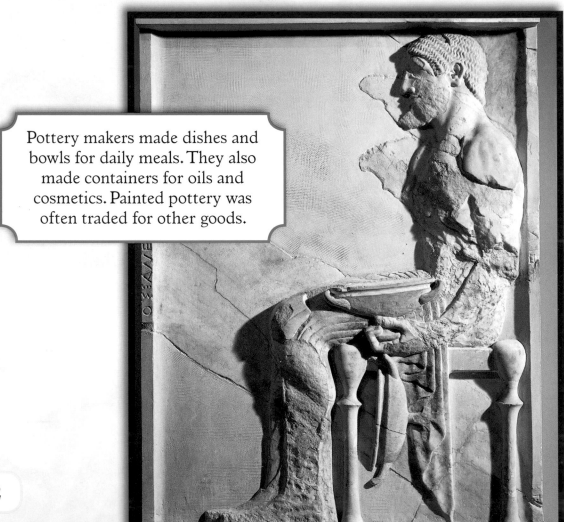

Pottery makers made dishes and bowls for daily meals. They also made containers for oils and cosmetics. Painted pottery was often traded for other goods.

This container is an example of black figure pottery. Greek pottery is important to historians because it often showed scenes of daily life in ancient Greece.

Pottery was made on a potter's wheel. The potter turned the wheel with his feet. Once a piece of pottery was created, it needed to be dried in a **kiln**. The potter could make pots with different colors by controlling how much air he let into the kiln. Pots dried in **oxygen**-rich air were red. Black or gray colors were dried with less fresh air around the pot.

The Importance of Pottery

One of the biggest industries in ancient Greece was pottery making. Greeks used the pottery in their daily lives. They used it to trade for goods they did not have as well. Greek pottery has been found in countries all over the world. This shows how well their trade system worked. They traded the

This red figure pottery showing a soldier could have been traded for many useful items.

pottery for raw materials, such as lead, iron, and bronze. They also traded it for foods they could not grow in their poor soil. They traded for other items, such as rugs, spices, and jewelry, too.

Not all pottery was painted as the example on the facing page was. These large clay pots at Knossos Palace in Crete are carved with designs instead.

Oils and Cosmetics

Creating and selling perfumes, cosmetics, and oils was another important business in ancient Greece. It was common for Greek woman to wear perfumes, oils, and cosmetics on their skin. Some cosmetics included eyeshadows and paints and skin glosses. Some people even dyed their hair.

This is an example of a pelike. A pelike is a two-handled container with a flat bottom. They were used to hold oils and other liquids.

This is a perfume bottle, also called an alabastron, that is in the shape of a person.

These products from ancient Greece were traded throughout the ancient world. The cosmetics and oils were stored in hand-carved shells from a clam common in the Red Sea. Later they were stored in pottery called *lekythoi,* which held up better during shipping. We know these items were important to Greek trade because these containers have been found in many places far from Greece.

At the Marketplace

The people of ancient Greece were busy growing food and making goods. Where could people go to buy the things they needed, though? They went to the marketplace, or agora, of course! The agora was an

These ruins of an agora are in Delos.

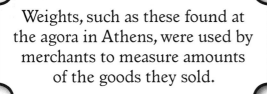

Weights, such as these found at the agora in Athens, were used by merchants to measure amounts of the goods they sold.

open-air market filled with people selling fish, oils and cosmetics, meats, pottery, cloth, tools, and regional foods.

Greek officials carefully watched trade in the agora. They made sure all the sellers were giving buyers a fair deal. They checked that weights and measures were standard. They also made sure all of the vendor's products were of good quality.

Trade

Greece is a peninsula and a group of small islands. People on the islands and the peninsula had different **resources**. They could trade these resources for goods they could not make on their own. They could also trade with other ancient civilizations around the Mediterranean Sea.

Greece would trade olive oil and wine for incense from Syria,

This map shows Greece and its neighbors. Some trade would have been done by traveling on land. Some neighbors would have been reached by sea.

This golden crown is from Sevasti, Greece. Jewelry like this was often used to trade.

Greece was surrounded by water and so fishing was another big industry. Places on the coast could trade fish for food or products that they did not have.

beef from Rome, rope and sails from Egypt, leather from North Africa, and cushions and rugs from Carthage. Much of what we have learned of ancient Greek economy and culture is known from the goods that have been found in places as far away as India, Spain, and Africa.

The Importance of Ships

Ancient Greece did a lot of trading with other countries. This meant they needed a lot of ships. Greece's shipbuilding industry built many kinds of ships. **Cargo** ships were the ones most often used in trade.

Triremes were a kind of battleship used in ancient Greece. These ships were used to keep trading vessels safe and to protect Greece's coasts from invaders.

Without boats, Greece's economy would not have been as rich as it was. We would not know nearly as much about ancient Greece without its overseas trade, either.

This postage stamp shows a ship that would have been used in ancient Greece.

GLOSSARY

artisans (AR-tih-zenz) A term for craftsmen or mechanics. People with a type of job that usually involves manual labor and the production or the repair of material items.

cargo (KAHR-goh) The load of goods carried by an airplane, a ship, or an automobile.

ceramics (suh-RA-miks) Made from matter, such as clay, that is heated until it hardens.

civilization (sih-vih-lih-ZAY-shun) People living in an organized way.

currency (KUR-en-see) Money.

kiln (KILN) An oven used to burn, to bake, or to dry something.

ore (OR) A natural solid material from which a metal or valuable mineral can be taken.

oxygen (OK-sih-jen) A gas that has no color or taste and is necessary for people and animals to breathe.

resources (REE-sors-ez) Things that occur in nature and that can be used or sold, such as gold, coal, or wool.

symbol (SIM-bul) An object or a picture that stands for something else.

INDEX

WEBSITES

Due to the changing nature of Internet links, PowerKids Press has developed an online list of websites related to the subject of this book. This site is updated regularly. Please use this link to access the list: www.powerkidslinks.com/sacg/econ/